Ministry's
NOT EASY

THE GUT WRENCHING, BLOOD, SWEAT AND TEARS
WAY TO BUILD A CHURCH

LEE ARMSTRONG

ISBN: 1460986113
ISBN-13: 9781460986110

Contents

Foreword

Pastor Lee is an anointed servant of God who is able to combine the knowledge and experience that he has gained over his years of ministry to equip and train church leaders and other ministry gifts to build great churches.

His experience for more than twenty-five years of ministry and training of our leadership teams has brought great insight and wisdom. There are numerous variables involved in building a healthy, functional and effective church. Pastor Lee has covered issues in twelve chapters that will bring success in leadership that will be pleasing to God. The impact and influence that Victory Life Church has had on thousands of congregants and multiple Victory Life locations is due, in large part, to the leadership of Pastor Lee. He has taught and lived the principles shared in this book and I believe, as you read and apply these same principles, you will be changed and equipped to be a part of a great church, as well.

Pastor Duane Sheriff
Senior Pastor
Victory Life Church/
Duane Sheriff Ministries
Durant OK

Introduction or Warning!
{You decide}

This book is an "in-your-face," Katy bar the door, politically incorrect book. If you're easily offended, read no further! If you are looking for a quick and easy way to build a successful ministry, stop now, because you will not find that formula here. The answers and truths in this book are often dependent on your ability to be patient, committed and on your willingness to endure the tests of character that are needed to be truly successful!

I have worked very hard to be as honest and transparent as I can be, without being belligerent and/or offensive (which became at times an almost impossible task). It was my earnest desire to share proven truths that quite frankly are not mentioned in other sources. I believe that has been accomplished without taking away from the truths shared in other places or venues.

In Christ,

Pastor Lee Armstrong
Victory Life Church/
Duane Sheriff Ministries

CHAPTER 1
Anointing is Never Enough
Ask Moses

Anointing is important and absolutely necessary, but it's never enough – just ask Moses! In Exodus 34: 29-35, Moses has spent time with God. The anointing is so strong on him that it's tangible. His face "shone." We might say it was glowing or shining with the glory of God! Few examples are as tangible and impressive as this encounter of an anointed man of God with his God. This, however, did not keep people from murmuring and complaining about his leadership style and his lack of providing for their wants and needs. It didn't keep those people who had been delivered from horrible bondage and slavery through his ministry from crying and wishing they had died in Egypt or in the wilderness. It didn't even keep his family and leadership team from criticizing his choice for a wife!

To further make the point, Jesus was the most anointed man of God to ever walk the planet, and yet it

wasn't enough to keep His leadership team from deny-
ing Him, or arguing with Him. It wasn't enough to keep
His enemies from stirring up opposition against Him,
and it wasn't enough to keep religious people from kill-
ing Him.

Now, I do not want to sound critical or unspiritual,
but we don't need the "double portion" as much as we
need to grow up and take ownership of our situations!
We need to realize we must grow if those around us are
to grow. We are responsible to develop good relationships, to build great teams, to make sure we are beyond
reproach with our finances, and that we are blameless
with our lives.

Let me share some of the roles that a Christian leader
should walk in, if he wants to truly be successful in ministry. He must be a true leader, an example to others, a
counselor, a business genius, a prophet, a team builder, a
manager, an encourager and a good communicator. He
must also be (at all times) a willing host, a hard worker,
a prayer warrior, a student of the Word, a teacher of the
Word, a motivational speaker, one who visits the widows,
goes to the hospital, the nursery, and a couple dozen other
things. This is hard work!

Jesus prayed often, but He still had to do the work.
His anointing did not make the work of the ministry
go away. He had to grow in wisdom and stature and in
favor with God and man. Maybe this is not the best of
examples, because most of us cannot comprehend that
Jesus was a man, all man, very man, really man. He ate
(God doesn't need to eat), He slept (God doesn't need
to sleep), and He died (God can't die)! Jesus was God

"come in the flesh." He therefore, was a man led by God. He was not God pretending to be a man. Jesus was not like Superman (who only pretended to be weak, but was really strong). He became fully human and in doing so, showed us how to live for God and do the work of the ministry. He showed us how to walk in the anointing of the Holy Spirit, and do miracles by living in obedience to His Heavenly Father.

Many Christian leaders are, as one man put it, "more annoying than anointed." This studious and sarcastic observation is truer than we would like to admit. It does, however, express my point very well. Being anointed will never replace the need to be kind, smart, or obedient to the voice of God. It will never override the Scriptural principle of "studying to show yourselves approved unto God," according to II Tim. 2:15. I know a pastor, very early in his ministry, who believed that if he just prayed that God would fill his mouth and he would be a preaching machine. He got up to speak and – surprise, surprise – he had nothing to say. This scenario is repeated in the lives of countless believers to one degree or another, individuals who have been taught to believe for the "double anointing, the double portion," and everything else will work out fine. Now I'm not trying to sound sarcastic or like I don't believe in the need for a true, genuine anointing from God. I just know we're often praying and believing for an anointing, when we *should* be *seeking* God – the same God Who spoke to the churches in Revelation about change; He wants to speak to *us* about change! He wants to speak to us about what we're doing right, as well as what we're doing wrong.

The same God Who anointed Moses also told Moses to appoint rulers, "over thousands, over hundreds, over fifties, and over tens," as in Deut. 1:15. This indicates that while they were anointed to lead, they still had varying abilities. In I Peter 4:10 -11, we are admonished to use the gift we've received from God, and this gift reveals His multi-faceted grace. The author also states that we are to minister through the ability that God gives us.

So, the bottom line is that the anointing is very real and very important, but it is not enough to fulfill your calling, or any other thing that God wants from you!

CHAPTER 2
It's Hard Work
The Four Letter Word

This is the four letter word of the Bible – "work." During His earthly ministry, Jesus worked hard – so hard, in fact, that John said if everything Jesus did was written in books, the world itself could not contain the books that should be written! *(John 21:25)*

No matter what the most recent spiritual guru tells us, building a church, with all its daily needs and ever-changing situations, is "hard work!"

The idea that we could build or even maintain a great church in some **quick and easy** way, is at best very dangerous and, at worst, not Biblical. There is no way that one can sit in the local diner, drinking lattés all morning and build a great church. Complaining about the people we have to work with or the "religious spirit" in our town won't get it done, either. What really takes away all our excuses concerning these problems is the revelation that everyone in the ministry has to deal with these same issues. We all have to work with the people God gives us, and we all have to deal with the religious spirit in our town, county or state! Think of it – from Adam to Jesus – they all had these same issues to deal with. Ministry would be easy if it wasn't for the people, the devil, and the devil in people!

Ministry – no wimps or cowards need apply! It is, and always will be, hard work. In today's anti-Christian, anti-Bible culture, it is even harder. This in no way means that we should give up, give in, or back down. It does mean, however, that we can't be deceived into believing that we can find a magical, mystical, or even spiritual micro-wave way to do what God's Word calls "work!"

Work is the nature and character of God. Gen.2:2 says, "And on the seventh day God ended his work which he had made; and he rested on the seventh day from all his work which he had made." When we work, we glorify and honor God, and we demonstrate that we are created in His image and likeness. This is exactly what Jesus said, "I have glorified thee on the earth: I have finished the work which thou gavest me to do." (John 17:4)

In Exodus 36:1-8, God gives us some wonderful truths about being in the service of the Lord. One of those insights is in verse 1 "...the Lord put wisdom and understanding to know how to work all manner of work for the service of the sanctuary." Notice how God gives us wisdom to work in the service of the Lord, and please take note that it's still called work. It's always been work, and it will always be work. Only God can give us the wisdom that we need to work in the ministry. And no matter how much wisdom you get, it's still work!

If you truly want to help people, it will not take very long for you to realize it's no easy task. It's hard work to help people change paradigms and mindsets that they have believed for many years. It's hard work, really hard work, to help anyone with an addiction, or lifelong problems, to get them to think new thoughts, to find new friends, and to start new habits that will become good behavior patterns to change their lifestyle.

In Num. 11:11-17, Moses became so exhausted with the weight of ministry, and the work of helping people, that he despaired of life and asked God to kill him! This is the man with the "rod of God." He was the man used by God to bring the Ten Commandments from God's presence to ours; he was the man God used to reveal His power to the Egyptians and the Pharaoh through the ten plagues; he was the man used to split the Red Sea, and then close it back up again. This is not a novice or babe in Christ, or some beginner in the things of the Kingdom. This is a true man of God, an anointed and appointed genuine man of God. But the pressure of helping people through the trials of life became overwhelming, even for him! God's answer to this problem was simple. God said that He would take the spirit to serve that was on Moses and put it on the leaders that Moses chose, so they could help "bear the burden of the people with him."

One of the greatest miracles in the entire Bible in my personal opinion is that of the rebuilding of "the wall of Jerusalem" described in the book of Nehemiah. They rebuilt these walls in an astounding 52 days. The real miracle is that there was no obvious miracle! God didn't send angels to move a single stone; there was no "rod of God," and no supernatural intervention. Nehemiah simply had a burden to rebuild the wall at Jerusalem and his passion convinced the king to help supply what was needed. Then Nehemiah persuaded the people to take ownership and responsibility to build whatever part of the wall they could - no more, no less. They did the work while standing guard against possible attack. At the risk of sounding sarcastic, the real miracle was that people actually worked! If you listen to many leaders today, they would have a prayer meeting and developed a "rebuild the wall committee." Then they would look at the demographics of the area, and then believe God to perform a miracle and "send someone else!" Sorry, but it has become common practice to pray and play, instead of becoming equipped to "do the work" of the ministry. There's one last note concerning the rebuilding of the wall. In chapter 3, the priest and the leaders were the first to start working! It does start from the top and works its way down.

In the New Testament, even what Jesus did in the ministry was called work. Mark 6:5 says "And he (Jesus) could there do no mighty work, save that he laid his hands upon a few sick folk, and healed them." See – ministry is work!

Jesus Himself called ministry work. John 4:34 says, "Jesus saith unto them, My meat is to do the will of him that sent me, and to finish his work." God calls it work in Acts 13:2 when it says, "As they ministered to the Lord, and fasted, the Holy Ghost said, Separate me Barnabas and Saul for the work whereunto I have called them."

There is just no getting around it – building a great church, being in the ministry on any leadership level, is work, and hard work at that! The good news is that if we do what God has called us to do, we are given grace to do it. We are therefore energized by the work, empowered by God, and equipped for the task. There's a beautiful truth revealed in Matt.11:28-30 where Jesus shows us His part in helping us with our work in the ministry. I will attempt to give you the "Readers Digest condensed version." Jesus said if we labor and are heavy laden, we should come to Him, and He'd give us rest (a refreshing). He goes on to say that if we will get yoked up with Him, and learn of Him, we will find rest for our souls. The word rest means recreation. We will find a vacation for our mind, will, and emotions. Now what happens to you when you're on vacation? Your whole attitude changes! It's not that there isn't any work during a vacation, but the work becomes a labor of love.

This is the promise of God when we become connected to Him. He said it this way: "Take my yoke upon you, and learn of Me." It is then we will act and feel like we are on vacation. I have personally experienced this and witnessed many others walk in this truth. Jesus said His yoke was easy and His burden was light. Therefore, if we are hooked up to Jesus, and listening to Him, it's like we're on vacation! Most people I know, while on vacation, work harder, get up earlier, go longer and farther, and even spend more money. The only difference is they're "on vacation!"

CHAPTER 3
THE #1 KEY
There is No KEY!

Two thousand pastors leave the ministry each month, according to one of the latest statistics. Additionally, eight out of ten pastors leave the ministry in their first five years. Most of their churches never fully recover from that decision. Many of those leaders fall into moral failure. Even more have stated they had no friends to open up to or be honest with. Still others say the main reason for leaving the ministry is the inability to resolve conflict. They were all looking for the "key" – to a successful marriage, ministry and so on. So, what *is* the key? What is the key to succeeding in the ministry and not falling into the traps that have kept so many from fulfilling their calling and God-given destiny?

It's one of the most commonly asked questions. "What's the key" to church growth, the key to increasing our church finances, the key to building a dynamic youth group, the key to having an incredible worship

11

team, and a hundred other things? The real problem is not the question per se, but the concept that there is one key and only one key to solve any of these problems. This idea is a myth that must be dealt with. The idea is crazy that there is some hidden key, some mystical ingredient or some three-step program, that if applied to our church, would make us grow exponentially. This myth is magnified by countless conferences and books that promote this idea, usually by asking people to come to their conference and buy their books. Almost every subject that you can think of these days has a book available with the words "quick and easy" in big bold letters in the title, implying and offering instant, almost overnight growth, and success.

This book is not one of those! Many readers will not even make it to the end of this book. This book is not meant for those looking for some quick and easy way to be successful in ministry. If it was easy, we would all have mega churches. The truth is there is no single truth, no single idea, and no simple prayer that will build your church into a mega church running 10,000 members by next month or even next year!

There are many variables involved in building a church of influence and impact. It would be impossible and impractical to try and list them all. For conversation and clarity, we will look at just a few.

For starters, there is your calling. Are you doing what God called you to do, what He gifted, and what He equipped you to do? Next, there are those leaders around you. Are they doing what God has called and gifted them to do? Then there is the simplicity of the number of people in your geographical area. If you are reaching 10% of your community, that number looks very different if your community is 10,000 strong or just 10! There's your style of preaching, your style of music. Do you start on time? What are your service times? How do you receive offerings? Are your greeters friendly? Where is your church located? Is it in town, out of town, or ten miles in the mountains, located next to a smelly factory? All of these things and hundreds more that could be mentioned, will have a direct and indirect impact on your success.

The point is, we need to stop trying to find the "quick and easy" microwave idea for building a great church. We simply need to roll up our sleeves and get to the work at hand. Jesus said *He* would build the church. Matt.16:18 says "And I say unto thee, That thou art Peter, and upon this rock I will build my church: and the gates of hell shall not prevail against it." The question we must ask ourselves is, "How did Jesus build the church?" The simple answer is, He gave His life for it, and He suffered and died for it. Look at the cross. It was the "gut wrenching, blood, sweat and tears way." If there was another way, He would have left it as our example.

Contrary to popular belief, building a church is not for wimps, and it's not for people who can't do anything else! It is hard work. It is a "gut-wrenching, blood, sweat and tears" vocation, but if it's God calling for you, it's a high calling, and the ultimate great adventure. Therefore, take full responsibility to pray and study, and to hear the voice of God saying, "This is the way, walk ye in it." (Is. 30:21) So, we gladly spend and are spent for others and the cause of Christ (II Cor. 12:15).

In Revelation, God speaks to seven different churches about what I like to call "the good, the bad, and the ugly" of those specific churches. He is very specific about their strengths, their weaknesses, and areas they needed to work on. This is very encouraging in one way and very scary in other ways. It is encouraging because God knows and cares about our church, and is willing to tell us "the good, the bad, and the ugly" about them. He doesn't do it in a condemning or belittling sort of way, but in a way that helps us fix those specific areas that need fixing. It's scary because it means we have to hear from God for ourselves, what areas we need to change and fix or keep doing. No one can do this for us. We must press in, we must know the voice of God, we must know what God is saying, and we must communicate the vision to others in a compelling, believable, and clearly defined manner. That is hard work!

Jesus said that He gave us the KEYS to the kingdom not the KEY to the kingdom! So, there is no single key, but multiple keys that we must be willing to change, tweak, or grow in our understanding and ability. Like most tasks that are relationship oriented, there is seldom just one key that would fix all our woes or problems. It does, however, bring to light, one very important key. That is, if we fix the problems that we DO know about, He will help us see other problems that we DON'T know about, that need our attention as well.

CHAPTER 4
Build Great Relationships
One is the Loneliest Number

A popular and very insightful song written in the 70's put these words to music, "One is the loneliest number you could ever do, two can be as bad as one, it's the loneliest number since the number one." (Harry Nilsson). This is true in ministry just as it is in life. If you're going to do anything great, or even semi-good, you're going to need help, and lots of it! I once read that if you're a leader, it's because others let you. I wholeheartedly believe it. This is a truth, and unfortunately, a truth that can't be ignored. One of the greatest hindrances to building truly great churches is the lack of building great relationships.

Even the Lone Ranger had Tonto! Too many pastors and leaders have a paradigm or perception that they are the only ones who can hear God, and the only ones able to do the work of God. This severely hinders how much God is able to do with them and through them. Let me demonstrate this through a simple example. If you had a family of ten children, would you find it difficult to keep up with them, and all of their activities? Most of us can't even keep up with the three or four children we have, and with all their various needs and activities – much less ten! Yet we ask a pastor to take care of a much larger family without even the slightest thought of how impossible this request really is. The good news is that help is available or at least on the way. The bad news is that the help is not perfect, not trained, and some are not even saved yet!

Can I share a hard truth with you and you not over-react to it? Here it is: people are crazy! Not just where you live and in your specific ministry, but everywhere. Here's another revelation. You and I are sometimes that crazy person in the life of someone else. We all have to use the people God sends us; the good, the bad, and the... well, you know the rest. Even Jesus worked with those who joined themselves to Him. Consider: Peter the one who denied Him, Thomas who doubted Him, and Judas who betrayed Him. One doesn't have to be a Bible scholar to see the motley crew that Jesus had around him. You know, the ones we now call disciples. They were not the spiritual elite or the great people of faith and power that we know they became. The process involved giving His life to them and for them. In Matt. 17:17, Jesus says, "... how long shall I be with you? How long shall I <u>suffer you?</u>" The word "suffer" means to put up with. That should help you believe and be thankful for the knowledge that God is fully aware of the difficulty you face working with others. In Heb. 4:15, our High Priest understands our situation and has been tempted like us, but He didn't sin!

I love the story of David and his mighty men that is told in II Sam. 23:8-23. Three of these mighty men are the men who risked their lives to bring David a glass of water from the well at Bethlehem. These three men faced entire armies and refused to back down, back up, or back away. I encourage you to read about these men and the others that are mentioned in this same chapter. It's very inspiring to know that people of this character and courage exist. Now be honest, aren't these the kind of people you long for? The kind of people who are armor bearers – who are so loyal and committed, that they would lay down their life for you. Don't you pray for God to surround you with the spiritual warriors who would fight their way through the enemy lines and back, just because you were down and needed some encouragement? Wow! Where do you get servants like that? I will tell you where, but you won't believe me even when I tell you. First, you sow them into existence. What you sow, you reap, remember? So the first thing you must ask yourself is, "Am I that dedicated to those over me? Have I been a warrior servant to my mentors?" Secondly, help will come from the same place David found it, in a cave, at one of the lowest points of his life, when he was desperate and in need of it. They found him in a cave.

Here's the problem with your help. They are in debt and of no financial help, they are in distress and no help bringing peace to the house, and they are discontented so nothing you do is going to be the right thing with them. That is not what you prayed for, or is it?

To really understand David's mighty men and their loyalty to him, we must go back to where David found them. "And every one that was in distress and everyone that was in debt, and every one that was discontented, gathered themselves unto him; and he became a captain over them: and there were with him about four hundred men." (I Sam. 22:2) Isn't this a great description of the body of Christ, or at least a description of many of those gathered around you? The reality of David's mighty men, and their unbelievable loyalty to him, is that David loved them when they were very needy people, and he helped them through those problems. He was willing to take them where they were and help them grow to their God-given potential. It takes great leadership skills, and a genuine love for people, to help them through these difficult problems. It's hard work, and there's no real shortcut, but the rewards can be your very own mighty men and women! Commitment and loyalty are gained the hard way, the old fashioned way – you earn it! You do this by serving others and helping them become all God intended them to be.

Let me show you the process of becoming a mighty man or woman of God. It's found back in I Sam. 16: 14-21. This is where David himself learned the process of becoming an armor bearer for himself. I will break this process down into four separate categories to help you see where we are with people, and where you need to go with them to get them to the next level in this process.

I Sam. 16:21 says, "And David came to Saul, and stood before him: and he loved him greatly; and he became his armourbearer." There it is, the process of becoming an armor bearer. Did you see it? It eluded me for years and then I saw it. The words "and he became his armourbearer" leaped off the pages at me. So I went back and studied hard to find some amazing things I would love to share with you.

The first truth in this process is simple, but life-changing. Here it is: Saul saw his need for others, and David came "when asked" to serve that need. Now I know what you're thinking. What's so powerful about that? Well, let me tell you. Most leaders are unwilling to ask for help! Now there are multiple reasons for this, some better than others, but all of them will be used against you in the long run. Some of the reasons include but, are not limited to: being hurt by people they've used in the past, being disappointed by the quality of other people's work, the lack of volunteers, and many others. This, how-ever, does not change the truth that you need others, and if you're going to accomplish the vision of God in your heart, you must learn to use those precious people in your care. If more leaders would just humble themselves and see their need for the gifts, talents, and strengths of others, God could do incredible things through them. This is harder than you would believe, because there's a trap, a mindset that comes with leadership. This trap is a concept, a thought that if you're the leader, or in charge, you are supposed to have all the answers; I am expected to be virtually invincible. So, asking for help would make me almost human – imagine that! The second part of this truth is the fact that people must respond to the call of God and the call of God's leaders. David heard the call from Saul for help and in essence said, "Yes."

The second truth revealed in this scripture is that David "stood before him." This indicates that he was there when Saul needed him. We have had many church "work days" since I've been a part of the local church, and we've never used anybody that didn't show up! I've gone through the entire Bible looking for insights on the qualifications for being used by God. I found two insights that changed my life. Here they are: God qualifies those He calls and He uses those who SHOW UP! There are so many people who are so much smarter, and far more articulate, and better looking than I, that it's embarrassing. The real reason I'm often chosen for a task by my pastor has much more to do with availability than it does with ability. I have often joked with our staff and other leaders that "I may not be the sharpest knife in the drawer, but I'm always in the drawer." This always gets a laugh, but it also makes my point. This does not mean I think I'm stupid, that I have a low self esteem, or that I have no skills. It just means the main reason I'm being used is – I showed up! So many people will say "call me if you need me," and while we should always be grateful for any help offered, the reality is that all too often it is just an empty promise. If however, you call and they are available, you should definitely take them up on their offer. Notice that David became his armor bearer, but he didn't start there!

The third truth in the "process of becoming" is that David "loved him greatly." Contrary to popular belief, there is no such thing as love at first sight. This idea makes for great romance novels and love songs, but it goes against Biblical truth. According to John 15:12, love involves commitment and sacrifice: "This is my commandment, that ye love one another, as I have loved you." The question that we must answer is "How did Jesus love us?" The answer is: He gave His life for us! And again in John 15:13, it says, "Greater love hath no man than this, that a man would lay down his life for his friends." This is what it means to "love someone greatly." This love has to be reciprocated for it to work. The leader has to love his co-workers, and the co-workers must love their leader "greatly." The king had to trust his armor bearer with his very life because in the heat of a battle, the armor bearer protected him from enemy attacks from behind. He was not in front of the king, but was to follow behind and fight the attacks that came from behind. Notice this in I Sam.14:12-13 where it shows this concept so clearly. "And the men of the garrison answered Jonathan and his armourbearer, and said, Come up to us, and we will shew you a thing. And Jonathan said unto his armourbearer, Come up <u>after me</u>; for the Lord hath delivered them into the hand of Israel." Then the response came in verse 13, "And Jonathan climbed up upon his hands and upon his feet, and his armourbearer <u>after him</u>: and they fell before Jonathan; <u>and his armourbearer slew after him</u>."

If more servants in the house of God would see the importance of protecting their leaders from the attacks that come from behind, we would see far fewer church splits. Also we would see fewer pastors throwing in the towel and giving up on their ministry. I've heard many people talk about how they were hurt by a pastor, and they probably were, but I've never heard a congregation repent for hurting their pastor. The attacks that came from behind involve, but were not limited to, murmuring and complaining, having a critical spirit, accusations and – well, you fill in the blank. With these enemy attacks, silence is not golden, it's deadly and dishonoring. Where are the armor bearers for the body of Christ today? Part of the reason I even considered writing this book is the potential to awaken many others to their God-given role as an armor bearer. If this strikes a chord with you, and you feel you would like to learn more on the subject of an armor bearer, please read the books "God's Armor Bearers" Volumes 1 and 2 by Terry Nance. His books on this subject keep me from reinventing the wheel. Visit his website at http://www.godsarmorbearer.com and order the books from his website. You would also benefit greatly from Pastor Duane Sheriff's (my Senior Pastor) series on **Armourbearers**. That series is available free of charge from Duane Sheriff Ministries. Feel free to visit them on the web at http://www.dsheriff.org/. There you will find all the information you need to order the free material available at the back of the book!

The fourth part of this "process of becoming" is that David "became his armourbearer." This simply means he didn't start there, and neither will you! It's a process, meaning that it takes time. There are things to be learned, character attributes to be developed (patience comes to mind), and truths to be gained in the process – so many that they can not be learned from a chalkboard. For instance, take forgiveness as an example. It is possible to learn Greek and Hebrew definitions for forgiveness, and actions of forgiveness, but forgiveness must be experienced from both sides to have a real working knowledge and understanding of it. This is the reason a young person may be extremely smart, but not know or be able to do what someone older can do or know. Experience teaches us things we could never learn in a classroom. Flying a plane is a good example of this. Would you rather have an inexperienced genius or a semi-intelligent, but experienced, pilot flying the plane you're in? Would you rather have the newly graduated brain surgeon, or the brain surgeon with 30 years of experience doing your procedure? That's what I thought. The good news is that this process is meant to benefit both the servant and the one being served. It gives each person involved time to develop a covenant relationship that endures the real battles of life and ministry.

CHAPTER 5
STAY HUMBLE
It's God Who Will Build His Church

Would you accept an award for being the most humble person in the world? If you did, would you still be the most humble person in the world? How you answer this question is very important. It reveals what you believe it means to be humble, and it's not what most of us have been taught. In Num. 12:3 the Scriptures say, "Now the man Moses was very meek, above all the men which were upon the face of the earth." Now the real eye-opener is that *Moses is the author who wrote those words.* So Moses said of *himself* that he was the meekest man on the earth. Jesus also said that He was meek and lowly of heart, in Matt.11:29. This flies in the face of what we've been taught a truly humble person would say of himself, doesn't it? Apparently God's idea of what it means to be humble must be different than ours. We must, therefore, seek to know what it means to be humble, in God's eyes, before we can begin "being humble."

Being humble is not to be confused with acting humble. Being humble comes from who you are; acting humble comes from what you'd like to be.

I had a teacher in Bible college who told his classes at the beginning of every semester that we needed to know two things: Number one, there is a God, and number two, you're not Him! That's what it means to be humble. It is the dichotomy of knowing we can do nothing of ourselves, but we can do all things through Christ, Who strengthens us. (Phil. 4:13). Having a low self-esteem is not synonymous with being humble. The Bible does not teach that we should "not think highly of ourselves;" as we've been taught. It teaches us that we should not think <u>more</u> highly of ourselves, than we ought to (Rom.12:3). The truth is God thinks *very* highly of you. He sent His Son to prove it. My pastor says it this way: "If God had a wallet, your picture would be in it." What a beautiful understanding of God's value and love for us.

It's very humbling to realize that for all our efforts, it is God Who builds His church. For us to brag about anything we did for God is like the axe bragging about cutting down a tree. At best, the axe was merely available for use. In essence, the best we can do is get out of the way and not mess up what God is doing! The Bible is extremely clear that the church is God's, the people are God's, and the Kingdom is His, not ours! Staying humble is so important to the success we can obtain and retain. So many leaders start out having true humility and a genuine dependency on God, but then begin to think it's by their own efforts that they are successful, or by their own strength they have what they have. This is so dangerous and there are so many warnings and examples of this mistake in the lives of God's people.

This is the whole reason for Gideon's army being reduced to a mere 300. Notice in Judges 7:2 "And the Lord said unto Gideon, The people that are with thee are too many for me to give the Midianites into their hands, lest Israel vaunt themselves against me, saying, <u>Mine own hand hath saved me</u>." They were still greatly outnumbered, but God wanted them to be totally dependant upon Him. He wanted them to know it wasn't their own strength that would win the battle. The only way to win was with God's help and hand.

The Scriptures are filled with stories of people who trusted God completely, and then, for a host of reasons, began to trust in their own efforts and abilities. In the book of Deuteronomy, chapter 8:1-20, God tells His people in verse 11, to "beware" that they don't forget the Lord their God. In verses 12-14 He says that, after they've "eaten and art full, and hast built goodly houses, and dwelt therein; And when thy herds and thy flock multiply, and thy silver and thy gold is multiplied, and all that thou hast is multiplied; Then thine heart be lifted up, and thou forget the Lord thy God, which brought thee forth out of the land of Egypt, from the house of bondage." This is something that happens to God's people way too often. They start out in complete faith, dependant on God, and then, somewhere along the way, they begin to walk in the flesh, trying to do God's will in their own strength and forget God. How many people or pastors do you know who were in church, praying and believing God for their business or churches to prosper, and when it happened, they were no longer in church or praying and studying as often? God is so awesome – He tells us the danger and trap that can come with His blessings, in slipping into pride and forgetting God; then He warns us not to fall into that trap.

Have you been through a wilderness experience? That time between promise and provision, where everything you believe is tested, and there are no simple answers to your questions? When you are in that wilderness, it seems like when you pray, the heavens are like brass. All the clichés are just that – clichés – where nothing seems to "work" for you. You fast and pray and all you get is hungry! If you haven't experienced this in your life as a Christian yet, you will. It is something that everyone I know and respect as a leader has experienced at some time in their life. The good news is – you can make it through this experience, and you can know why you're going through it.

The Bible teaches us that the wilderness experience has six main truths to teach us. Let's look at these in Deut. 8:2, 3 and 5: "And thou shalt remember the way which the Lord thy God led thee these forty years in the wilderness…" In modern day English:

1) <u>To humble you</u>
2) <u>To prove you</u>
3) <u>To know what was in your heart</u>
4) <u>To know if you would keep His commandments or not.</u>
5) <u>That you would know, that man lives by every word that comes from God</u>
6) <u>God chastens us like a father does his son.</u>

The wilderness is not meant to be in vain or unprofitable. It is a time in your life for God to accomplish these six things. So don't do as others have done and harden your heart towards God. Instead, learn the lessons and truths that will bring you into your promised land.

In 1st *Peter 5:5*, we read in the latter part of the verse "... for God resisteth the proud, and giveth grace to the humble." Wow! Can you imagine this concept? If you're in pride, God becomes your opponent. You are literally fighting with God, and we all know that the only way to win a battle against God is to lose. Think about it – if God wanted to, He could flick His finger and send us to the next universe. In James 4:6, there is a phenomenal revelation that we must look at. It will ruffle some of our traditional teachings about grace, but we will all be grateful for the knowledge afterwards. Let's read the verse: "But He giveth more grace. Wherefore he saith, God, resisteth the proud, but giveth grace unto the humble." There it is: He giveth <u>more grace</u>.

Now I've been taught most of my Christian life that grace is "God's unmerited favor" and while grace does include unmerited favor, it is not limited to that alone. How do I know? God will give you more of it! If it's just unmerited favor, how can you get more of it? Thank God the Scriptures clarify what grace is, according to God, and why we need and can get more of it. The apostle Paul was under attack from Satan, and he asked God to take it away. Here's what God told him, "...My <u>grace </u>is sufficient for thee: <u>for my strength is made perfect in weakness</u>." (II Cor.12:9). What a powerful definition of grace! According to God, grace is defined as "His strength where we are weak" – that is why we can get more of it. When we recognize we are weak in an area and humble ourselves, God gives us more grace, more of His strength in that area where we are weak! This is why God can say His grace is sufficient. He wasn't saying, "Just suffer through and deal with it as best as you can," which is what most of us have been taught. However, He did say, "I'll be your strength in areas where you are weak." The more we recognize and admit our weaknesses, the more grace God gives us! When we humble ourselves, God exalts us. "And whosoever shall exalt himself shall be abased; and he that shall humble himself shall be exalted." (Matt.23:12) There it is again, God resists the proud but gives grace to the humble. Always remember that promotion in the kingdom does not come from the east or the west (natural things), but from the Lord (Psalms 75:6-7).

"Whosoever therefore shall humble himself as this little child, the same is the greatest in the kingdom of heaven." (Matt.18:4) There's not much we can add to that is there? It's pretty self-explanatory. Jesus is the greatest in the Kingdom, for many reasons, but one of the main reasons is because He humbled Himself more than anyone ever humbled themselves! He gave us an example of how to truly be successful in God's kingdom-be humble!

CHAPTER 6
GROW UP
When You Were a Child

Jesus is coming back for a bride, not a child! The Church of Jesus Christ must grow up! In I Cor.13:11, Paul says, "When I was a child, I spake as a child, I understood as a child, I thought as a child: but when I became a man, I put away childish things." This reveals some very interesting thoughts about growing up. We see that there is a time when it's proper to be a child. Paul said "when I was a child" not "if I were a child." Jesus was a child, but He grew in wisdom and in stature, and in favor with God and man (Luke 2:52). It is quite normal to be in diapers when you're a child, but if you are still in diapers when you are fifteen, something's not as it should be. You didn't grow up properly; something stunted the natural growth pattern. So we see growing up is God's plan and desire for us, our people, and our churches.

In many ways, growing up naturally corresponds with growing up spiritually, and this was Paul's point. If we will stick with this idea, many things become almost self-explanatory. Paul said that when we were children, we spoke as children. You almost have to have help to miss it! As a child, we said many cute things, but we lacked wisdom and understanding; our hearts were right, but what we said was not very intelligent. I understand this because I'm a grandfather and I absolutely love it. My grandchildren are such a delight, and they say some of the cutest things! But because they're children, what they say is wonderful. It wouldn't be so wonderful if they are still saying those things when they're 20! As a new babe in Christ, we often say things that are less than intelligent (cute), but lacking the wisdom gained only by growing up.

I know a man who, shortly after being born again, was told about counting it all joy when you fall into "divers temptations" from James 1: 2. He was glad to know that divers had temptations, but wanted to know what that had to do with him; he wasn't a diver. These instances are often humorous when we're new to the things of the Kingdom. They are at best disheartening when we are no longer babes in Christ.

We see that the natural realm often points to and speaks of the supernatural realm. Just like the natural growth of a man or woman is needed and necessary, it is also needed and necessary for the servants of the Lord. We must grow up and start talking like adults, like people of maturity. Mature Christians are not continually whining, or murmuring and complaining; they're not possessive, crying "It's mine, mine, mine," but rather they're encouraging others, speaking the truth, and seasoning their words with grace.

One last thought before we move on. We must be sure to season our words with grace – maybe chew on them for a while, before spitting them out, because words are sown and therefore reaped. We will have the opportunity to eat those words again. As mature Christians, we need to understand this and speak our words with caution and compassion!!

Our understanding changes as we grow up. We should no longer believe in the Easter bunny, Santa Claus, and the Tooth Fairy. We no longer believe that a stork brings our baby brothers and sisters to us. Our understanding of life and death, and everything in between is based on how much truth we can handle. However, some Christians never seem to move past the initial born-again experience. Salvation is the starting line, not the finish line. This is not to take away from the importance of salvation, but if the message of the Bible was to get saved, and that was the ultimate goal, then we should get people saved and then hit them on the head before they can backslide and mess up! I hope that's not too hard, and that you don't think badly of me for saying it. I obviously don't recommend this kind of behavior, or suggest it as a course of action. I'm only trying to magnify the mistake of thinking that there's nothing more to Christianity than salvation.

Notice Prov.23:7, which says, "For as a man thinketh, in his heart, so is he." We are what we think we are, according to the Scriptures. If we change what we think, we change what and who we are! Everything begins and ends with our thought life. In simplicity, here's the process: you have a thought, that thought becomes an action, that action becomes a habit, that habit becomes a lifestyle, and then your lifestyle leads to your thought life! Let me share with you a life-changing Biblical truth. Our battle is in our minds, and in our thought life, and not with people, according to II Cor.10:3-5. Starting with verse 3, "For though we walk in the flesh, we do not war after the flesh: (For the weapons of our warfare are not carnal, but mighty through God to the pulling down of strong holds;) Casting down imaginations, and every high thing that exalteth itself against the knowledge of God, and bringing into captivity every thought to the obedience of Christ." We win or are defeated in a spiritual battle by the things we're thinking on! Now this is no walk in the park; it's "a battle." Let me prove it. Try this thought control exercise:

Don't think of a red-faced monkey. Don't do it! Stop it! Come on now, I mean it, stop thinking about it.

How'd you do? Don't tell me, I know how you did; you failed. Why? You failed because the strength of sin is the Law. The more you try not to think about something, the more you think about it.

The only way to "not think" about something, is to think about something else. We need to think on what the Bible tells us to think on. For instance, Phil. 4:8 tells us to think on the things that are, true, honest, just, pure, lovely, of a good report, things that are virtuous, and praiseworthy. The result is in verse 9 "... and the God of peace shall be with you." But notice what happens when we think on negative things. "Men's hearts failing them for fear, and for looking after those things which were coming on the earth..." (Luke 21:26) Now let's go back to II Cor. 3:11 and continue looking at the process of growing up.

Paul says, "When I became a man, I put away childish things." Notice he didn't say "If" I become a man but "when" I became a man, I put away childish things. It's expected by God that we grow up. Becoming a man is a process; it's more than any single event, like turning eighteen, or getting a car, or even a job. All these things can be a part of the maturing process, but none of them can make us mature on their own. Maturity in the Kingdom of God is no different; there will be no single event that happens and suddenly people call you mature. We all know people who have been serving God for forty years and still have very little maturity in their Christian walk, and still others who are fairly new in the Kingdom, but demonstrate genuine maturity.

Here are seven signs of maturity, according to Ephesians, chapter 4:

1) We're willing to work in the ministry. (verse 12)
2) We edify the body of Christ. (verse 12)
3) We're no more children. (verse 14)
4) We stay with solid doctrine. (verse 14)
5) We speak the truth in love. (verse 15)
6) We supply others and we are supplied by others. (verse 16)
7) We bring increase to the body. (verse 16)

Now let's take a closer look at these, and allow God to speak to us.

1) Children don't like to work! Adults don't either, but we do it anyway. Why? We are mature, and we understand that's what adults do.

2) Children have a hard time boasting and bragging on others. So do adults who are not secure in their own skin and with who and what God has made them. As mature Christians, we think more highly of others than of ourselves.

3) Children don't like responsibility. As adults, we know that's not an option. Responsibility is the cost of maturity

4) Children are easily persuaded; grown-ups are not so easily convinced. Life's experiences have taught them to be convinced and convicted. Solid doctrine is so vital to being grown up!

5) Children speak the truth with no regard or understanding of how it may hurt another. "You have a big nose, you're fat…." As mature adults, we speak the truth in love! We understand that speaking the truth without love can hurt more than it can help.

6) Children just want to be supplied (give me, can I, I want). When we grow up, we look for opportunities to give to others. We really enjoy using our gifts and talents to serve others!

#7) Children are often good at tearing things down, but seldom any good at building things up. As adults, however, we have learned to put things together by reading the instruction manual, i.e., the B.I.B.L.E. which is an acronym for "Basic Instructions Before Leaving Earth." As mature Christians, we add to the body of Christ. We add value to the whole – with our presence, with our gifts and talents, with our finances, and by bringing others into the church!

CHAPTER 7
COMMITMENT
To Him That Endureth

Our commitment is to the Kingdom of God, and not our own! Rev. 2:26 says "And he that overcometh, and keepeth my works <u>unto the end</u>, to him will I give power over the nations." In talking about the sower, Mark tells us, "And these are they likewise which are sown on stony ground; who, when they heard the word, immediately receive it with gladness; "And have no root in themselves, <u>and so endure but for a time: afterward, when affliction or persecution ariseth for the word's sake, immediately they are offended</u>." (Mark 4:16-17).

We all know people who once followed the Lord, even some pastors – individuals who could not endure, for whatever reason. I'm not casting stones nor am I making excuses; most of these individuals have been really beaten up and are genuinely hurt. What they didn't know is that when they got saved and started to serve the Lord, they entered a war zone! This is why commitment is so important. There is a real enemy whose sole purpose is to keep us from our destiny, to steal, kill and destroy! It's not a game, and if we are not serious about the Kingdom and the things of God, the enemy of our soul will cause us to throw in the towel.

It has been said that it's not how we start a race, but how we finish that counts. Paul said in II Tim. 4:7 "I have fought a good fight, I have finished my course, I have kept the faith." That's the way to live and die as a disciplined follower of Christ. Fight a good fight, finish what God has given us to do, and keep the faith. If what you're doing is not worth dying for, it's not worth living for, either! It is so easy to get wrapped up in good things that are not God things! I personally believe that many of these things are meant to wear us out, so we will not have the energy to do the things God truly wants us to do.

If you know God called you, and you're doing what you know He called you to do, then you will lay down your life for it, and you will do it with joy. Jesus endured the cross and all that came with it, for the JOY that was set before Him (Heb. 12:2). He knew that what He was doing was in the will of God, and it was generational. The joy that was set before him (at least in part) was you and me with Him, for eternity! Jesus showed us that He was able to stay the course, because He was committed, not only to the temporal, but to generations yet to come. If we understand commitment properly, we will see that commitment helps build something of significance now, and lays a foundation for others to build upon and hopefully improve upon. God is, and He wants us to be, generational in our thinking. The Scriptures prove this to be true many, many times. Let me give just a few Scriptural examples. "For he said, because the Lord hath sworn that the Lord will have war with Amalek (a type and shadow of sin) <u>from generation to generation</u>." (Exodus 17:16) "... but my righteousness shall be for ever, and my salvation <u>from generation to generation</u>" (Isaiah 51:8), and just one more, "And his mercy is on them that fear him <u>from generation to generation</u>." (Luke 1:50)

If you think generationally about vision (and you should, because God does), your ministry now and your future ministry becomes very exciting. It's exciting because what you're doing can now be seen as a springboard and a catalyst for the next generation of leaders, which could catapult them into being more fruitful than you! If, however, you're building your ministry to showcase how gifted you are, and how much better you are than others like you, this is **not** good news. Far too many leaders are afraid to empower others and help others become great. They feel it would make them look less gifted and less like a great leader. The truth is, if you are gifted enough to help develop genuine leaders, heroes in the faith, you will be considered a great leader like John Wooden, John Maxwell, Mother Teresa. These leaders have mentored and motivated many others by their willingness to commit themselves to developing others. So what is their legacy? They're all known and honored as great leaders.

What does it take to mentor great leaders? Only a lifetime of commitment!! Jesus gave His life so His followers could see His commitment to them and their destiny, and so will you, if you want to leave a generational legacy. This is hard work and must be done intentionally; it doesn't just happen by osmosis or because we wish it to. Like raising children, developing others must be done by choosing everyday opportunities and intentional encounters that we create on purpose (pun intended).

One of my favorite stories in the Old Testament is where King David wanted to build a temple for the Ark of the Covenant, but God said no (1st Chron. 28:2). Have you ever heard God say no to anything you really wanted to do? It can be very hard to deal with. Not only that, God tells you someone else is going to do what was in your heart to do. It was his son Solomon, but that could be even worse at times. Yet look at David's response; he tells Solomon what he heard God say, and then gives him what in today's economy would be equivalent to millions of dollars to help make it happen. That's generational thinking; that is called a true commitment to God's kingdom not his.

I love investing in others; that's just a part of the purpose for writing this book. The thought that I might be able to help mentor someone who will do what I can't, or maybe what I can, but better, really does excite me! Here's a thought-provoking statement: "Verily, verily, I say unto you, He that believeth on me, the works that I do shall he do also; and greater works than these shall he do; because I go unto my Father." (John 14:12). Jesus sowed into his disciples and commited to them with a strong belief that they would do not only what He did, but that they would do even greater. Remember, our commitment is to God's Kingdom, not ours! His kingdom is from generation to generation!

CHAPTER 8
BE HONEST
The Best Policy, But It Sure Isn't Easy

"**G**et thee behind me Satan, thou art an offence unto me: for thou savourest not the things that be of God, but those that be of men" (Matt. 16:23). How's that for honesty? We can't even offer someone a breath mint without creating a major conflict. How about, "…O faithless and perverse generation, how long shall I be with you? how long shall I suffer you?" (Matt. 17:17) The word "suffer" here means to put up with. These statements were made to His disciples, His friends; He was even harder on the religious Pharisees and Sadducees. He called them "vipers" and "hypocrites," and even called them "whitewashed sepulchers, full of dead men's bones." Not very complimentary, but HONEST! I love the fact that God is not interested in being politically correct; He **cannot** lie and neither should we. The honesty of the Scriptures is so refreshing to me. God does not allow us to use the color of our skin, what side of the tracks we were born on, or even our parents, as a reason for being like we are. He states emphatically that our problem is not that we were born in the wrong place, but rather that we were born in the first place. That is, we were born a sinner, straight from the womb. None of us had to be taught to sin – it came to us quite naturally. We could lie, place blame, and manipulate before we even understood these actions. So God cuts through all the lies we might be inclined to use as an excuse for our life, and tells us plainly the problem is US!

The Bible tells us that knowing the truth will set us free; this means that lies, all lies big or little, put us in bondage. It further means when we are not honest with ourselves and others, we create areas of bondage for us and for them. So many ministries will fall far short and not reach their full potential because they have never learned the power of being truly honest with people. Honesty is always the best policy, but it isn't easy! However, it is the only way to build great relationships and a great church, but it's not easy. It's not easy to tell someone they can't sing, or they don't have the skills or giftings to fulfill a particular aspect of ministry. This gets even more complicated if the other leaders in their life (past and present) have not been as honest with them about these same issues. All of us have experienced dealing with people who have good hearts, but they're working hard at something they shouldn't be doing, and are not gifted to do: administrators who can't administrate, singers who can't sing, preachers who can't preach. On and on we could go, the list is endless – just fill in the blank. This problem is multiplied exponentially if these individuals are related to us. Many leaders have taken what looks like the easy way out (avoidance) and let things go much longer than they should have, in an attempt to keep peace, hoping the situation will just resolve itself and will go away. The question is, has that approach ever truly worked out in the long run? If we're honest, we know it hasn't; it only prolongs and often increases the pain.

When we are forced to address the real problem (and believe me, we will have to deal with it eventually), we realize the issue is far worse now and more people are involved than if we had just dealt with the problem and been honest in the very beginning. I said this wasn't going to be a book of easy simple solutions.

Working with real people with real problems is very complex and often exhausting. Few people are good at conflict resolution, because most of us have never been taught how to deal with these kinds of problems. I don't know about you, but in the Bible school I went to, and in all the books I've read, no one told me that "sheep bite" really hard! We have been taught that conflict is always related and/or connected to sin, so our response is to avoid conflict at all cost. The problem with this approach is that it becomes a self-fulfilling prophecy. That's exactly what happens; it costs us a lot more than we really wanted to pay, but pay we will. The good news is, it costs less if we deal with it early!

* * *

Remember the old saying from the commercial, "You can pay me now, or you can pay me later"? It was about buying an oil filter for a few dollars now, or paying for a complete engine rebuild which costs thousands of dollars later. The point is dealing with someone early may hurt, but not as much as if we wait. It's never easy, but the only way to grow or get better at something is for the leaders we trust to be honest with us about our strengths and weaknesses. I believe everyone's a "ten" at something and our job as leaders is to help them find out what that "something" is. When leaders do what God has designed and purposed for them to do, it's a beautiful thing, and it glorifies God. Notice again what Jesus said in John 17:4, "I have glorified thee on the earth: I have finished the work which thou gavest me to do." We all have a work that God has for us to do, and when we do it, we glorify God. That's why we must be honest with those wonderful people God has placed in our care. They deserve to find what glorifies God in their lives as well.

Being truly honest with people is not the same as being rude, mean, or what some call brutally honest. The scripture teaches that we are to speak the truth in love. That means love is the motivation for us being honest. It is not love to lie to people; it may be easier for the moment, but it's not love, and it's not biblical. The goal should never be to let people leave church, but to help them find their nitch, their seat on the bus, their line in the play, their note in the song, or whatever we want to call it. Sometimes that does mean we have to let them go, but it should never be our first response.

There are countless individuals who are seriously wounded and are no longer in the ministry because leaders mishandled them. The leaders waited until there was so much contention and strife in the situation that termination was the only recourse. Things were said and done that were very painful, and even worse maybe beyond repair. There was no honest dialog about what was done right and what was done wrong. I have seen people work for ministries and getting good monthly revues, only to be let go at the end of the year. That's not the worst of it, they were let go for something other than the truth. Instead of saying we were not honest with you about your monthly reviews, and you didn't do what we agreed upon, or whatever the real issue is, some false reason is given. This is unethical, immoral and unbelievable, all at the same time. No one wins, no one learns, no one grows. It takes real maturity and genuine love for people to be honest with them, and I have found by experience that most people respect leaders who will speak the truth to them in love. This doesn't mean it's easy or that it won't cause conflict, it just means even if they disagree with you most still respect you for being honest.

Jesus said, "Thou hypocrite, first cast out the beam out of thine own eye; and then thou shalt see clearly to cast out the mote out of thy brother's eye" (Matt. 7:5). Being honest with others works best when they see that we are willing to be honest about ourselves. If we will first admit we are not Superman, it makes it easier for others to admit they're not Robin! It is a truly liberating day when we realize it's all right, and often the right thing, to say "I don't know", or "I can't do that". Remember, knowing the truth shall set you free; you're free because you know you have limitations. What's really encouraging is when you realize that what you can't do, someone else does very well, and they actually enjoy it! I know there's a teaching by many leaders that promotes not letting anyone see your weaknesses, or not letting them too close to you because they will loose respect for you. I hate to be the one to break this to you, but they already know you have weaknesses, and if you choose to believe in not letting people close to you, that is when you will loose their respect.

I love the Apostle Paul's honesty about his personal struggles with the flesh. He tells us in Rom. 7:19 "For the good I would I do not: but the evil which I would not, that I do." Wow, what honesty. In modern day English, Paul said, "I don't do the good I want to do, and the bad I don't want to do, that's what I do". I think we can relate to Paul's real life struggles, and because of his being truthful about it, we can identify with him; therefore we are encouraged to be this honest with others about our weaknesses. We realize we are not the only one with issues, and that even our most famous heroes of the faith have chinks in their armor (every last one of them)! It is one of the beautiful things I have grown to love about the Bible, the honest descriptions of God's men and women. The truth about Moses and his anger, David and his lack of self control, and even Paul and Barnabus having so much contention over John Mark that they separated company over it. This should be such a comfort to us, knowing God uses those who show up, and that no one is or was flawless, except Christ.

The scriptures are clear that Jesus our high priest knows how we feel, and understands and he sympathizes with us. He's not condemning us or belittling; He's been there done that, and so He understands us. This allows us to be open and honest with God and not have any fear of being rejected by him. I admit it's not quite as easy to be that open and honest. Some are more than willing to reject you, or worse than that, use your honesty against you. This, however, does not make null and void the need for us to be transparent and open with people. It just means we will have to be honest with them about the situation and leave it, between them and God.

CHAPTER 9
Deal with Conflict
Whom the Lord Loveth

Conflict is not probable or even possible, it's inevitable and necessary! Jesus walked in perfect love, wisdom, justice and judgment, and yet, He had conflict everywhere He went. The servant is not greater than the master; if they hated Him they will hate us. The Word of God is so clear about this: "Yea, and all that will live godly in Christ Jesus shall suffer persecution" (II Tim. 3:12).

We will look at two separate kinds of conflict: that which comes from being a Christian and that which happens between Christians! In II Cor. 6:14-18, Paul makes it plain that in certain situations as a Christian, conflict is necessary and appropriate. Light and darkness, righteousness and unrighteousness, Christ and the Devil, will always be in conflict with each other, always! This conflict is needed; it is a must if we expect our lives to have impact. Until we live a life worth dying for, no one will ever believe it's worth living for. Jesus lived His life totally obedient to His heavenly Father, and what was the response of those around Him? Conflict or conversion, revival or riot, they loved him and they hated Him, believed He was of God, and believed was full of the devil. It will be no different for you! People you've never even met hate us today just because we're believers! Everything Jesus did caused conflict: who He ate with, whose house He went to, that He ate at all, and because He healed someone on the wrong day. He never apologized for the conflict He created by doing what was right, and neither should we.

The politically correct and the moral relativists will just have to deal with our presence and our preaching because we're not going to be tolerant. Tolerance is a philosophy for cowards! It stands for nothing and therefore falls for everything. If we believe something, really believe it; that belief, by its very definition, puts us in contrast to those with other beliefs. Tolerance is not for the Christian whose life changing truths are in the face of everything the tolerant crowd call dear; it can get us killed! The Pharisees of our time will hate us and what we stand for just as much as they did Jesus.

This is a part of the Christian experience, because we are at war against all things that God calls unrighteous. Notice the language of the scriptures and you can't miss this idea. Paul said "fight the good fight", "Put on the whole armor of God", "we wrestle not against flesh and blood", "endure hardness as a good soldier", and many other scriptures show us that because we are at war, conflict is necessary and needed.

The other kind of conflict, "that which is between believers," is also inevitable, but should be walked out differently, until resolution is accomplished. If we're honest, there is conflict in almost every relationship we have. I'm really surprised we don't have more murders in marriage than we do! We put two people, who are complete opposites, together in a house and say "survive." One likes it hot in the house, the other likes it cold; one likes a fan on high, the other wants no fan at all; ones an early riser, the other a late morning person; one drives from the driver's side, the other from the passenger side; get the picture?

Conflict is a part of all relationships and has little to do with our love for one another, but, is based on our differences. Men and women will always have conflict because "they are different"; parents and children will always have conflict; you and those that you're connected to you will always have conflict, "because you're different". This, however, is not to be treated the same as the conflict between light and darkness, righteousness and unrighteousness. We are to work things out with our brothers and our sisters. Through forgiveness, repentance, and open, honest dialog we are to resolve conflict with each other. The problem is we avoid conflict for many reasons, but not one of the reasons will fix the problem (refer to the last chapter).

I want to share with you an eye opening, and not so well known truth. Conflict has a purpose, and that purpose is at least two fold.

First, realize conflict is a doorway to intimacy; yes intimacy. My pastor defines intimacy this way, "into-me-see", and that is exactly what is revealed in conflict. We are looking into that person's heart and mind, and seeing something we didn't see before. Few people create conflict on purpose; it is the by-product of touching an area of the heart that demands a response. Have you ever been talking to your spouse and then you get "the look"? You know, that look that lets you know you're in trouble. We all know that look, and if we are smart we will ask them what they heard us say, not just what we thought we said. That look is because what we said and what was heard were two different things. What they heard touched a hurt, a pain, a past situation that resulted in conflict, the look. This is the doorway to intimacy, mentioned earlier, that has a purpose. Here is where so many of us miss the mark (sin). We get angry or frustrated and we start arguing instead of seeking the real issue.

Most people don't get up in the morning and say I'm going to be an angry, unmanageable person today! They are the sum total of the influence of people and things: siblings, friends, classmates, books, movies, music, and hundreds of other things-good, bad and ugly. These influences are the baggage that we all bring to every new relationship we are exposed to. If you've had bad encounters with those in authority, you will bring that mindset into every relationship, subconsciously or not. This will either be confirmed or challenged by the future authorities in your life.

I personally spend the majority of my time with new members of the ministry, proving to them I'm not like the leaders in their pasts. This is much harder than working with those who have never been abused by other leaders.

If I say or do something that reminds them of past abuse by previous leadership, they will recoil and wait for the abuse, and so will those in your ministry. We must recognize this is a natural defense mechanism that they have come by honestly. Like the animal that's been beaten by its previous owners, it will take loving patience to teach them we can be trusted. It's very enlightening to discover that the trainers of theme park animals spend as much as two years teaching those animals "they can be trusted". Long before anything of real value can be asked of the animal, trust must be established. I believe, and so does God, that people are much smarter than any theme park animal, and much more deserving of the time needed to prove we can be trusted, before we ask anything of real value out of them as well! Then, and only then, can we see conflict as a doorway into helping people instead of creating further hurt.

The second purpose for conflict is best described by a simple real life example. If you've ever watched a baby chicken hatch out of an egg, you've seen the reason. Watching this event is almost painful because the small chicken has to peck his way out of the shell from the inside out. He starts pecking very frantically and with great effort. He stops and breaths in an almost hyperventilating manner and then starts the arduous task of pecking again; however if, because you can and or because you feel sorry for the chicken, you help the chicken out of the shell, he will, at best, be born crippled or he will die! This is because God has created the conflict of getting out of the shell to prepare the chicken for life outside the shell. Many of the things you've had to endure, the conflicts of your life, those situations that made no sense, while painful and extremely difficult have prepared you to endure outside of your shell! If you will but look at many of today's generation you will see the results of making life easier for them.

Many parents have believed the psychobabble of the so-called experts and made their children's happiness the goal of life. They did everything possible to remove any kind of pain, hardship, difficulty or conflict, from their lives. The result is a generation of emotionally crippled and spiritually dead chickens! These individuals won't get a job, they won't work on relationships, and they won't even take the responsibility of raising their own children. They've become selfish, self-centered, and are unable to endure any conflict whatsoever. Sound like anybody you know? This is not meant to excuse or accuse anyone. I share it merely to awaken us to the purpose and benefit of conflict in our lives.

CHAPTER 10

What, Where, When, Who, and Why?

"**A**nd the Lord answered me, and said, Write the vision, And make it plain upon tables, that he may run that readeth it" (Hab. 2:2). I have seen that most of our frustrations and problems in ministry are not because of the devil. It is, in simplicity, a lack of clarity and understanding. Clarity is so vital to the growth of any ministry or business. I read recently that the number one motivation of people is not money, but rather communication, and surprisingly, communication about the good, bad and the ugly! Money is not the great motivator that we've been led to believe. In reality it only motivates people for about three weeks. Anyone dealing with finances and seeing how people respond to a raise knows this to be true.

I think all leaders need to read Ken Blanchard's book, **The One Minute Manager**, because he shares the need for communication and clarity so well. For those who won't read the book let me explain a simple truth from it.

We all need to know how to score "a win" in our job. We need a clear idea of what it looks like to win the game, or at least score so we can please the coach. In bowling the win is to knock all the pins down as often as you can, and because you know this truth, you and all those around you celebrate when you score a strike! But if you didn't know how to score, the response would be that of frustration, and yet, as incredible as it sounds that is exactly how most people do their job. This is also true in ministry. This is because with the ministry our job descriptions are way too often very ambiguous, generic and not really clear. For example what is the job description for most youth pastors? Grow the youth group into godly men and women. The problem is obvious and apparent. What, where, when, who, and why are completely missing in this description. What's worse is the pastor probably couldn't answer all those questions even if he were asked. They are then held accountable for not doing what was not made clear to them! So, the conversation goes something like this. (Leader) "Why didn't you go see sister "what's her name"? (Servant) "I didn't know that was a part of my job". (Leader) "What do you mean you didn't know it was a part of your job, you're the youth pastor"! (Servant) "She's not in our youth group". (Leader) "But she should be."

This is so common that many of you reading this book have experienced similar conversations. We are often so desperate for help that we will bring someone on the team and then fill in the blanks as we go. This is not only wrong, it is frustrating for everyone involved. In my humble opinion, we need several interviews with the same candidate before they are hired. We, as a whole, hire people too quickly and let them go too slowly. Our hearts are right, but our thinking is flawed; we owe it to ourselves and others to spend more time being clear and thorough from the beginning; we will then save ourselves much hurt and pain.

Let me finish with this wonderful example of how to be sure your instructions are clear. I read about a high-ranking officer who, during his tenure at war, would give his instructions to an intellectually-challenged individual, and if that individual could repeat and understand those instructions, he knew his instructions were clear and could be followed. What a lesson we could all learn from this example. Write your instructions down, MAKE THEM SO CLEAR, that those around you can understand the vision!!

CHAPTER 11
Lead
Leaders Lead

You can manage money, systems, machines and even your time, but people do not want to be managed!! They want to be released and encouraged to use their God given gifts for the glory of God, and they are looking for a leader who will lead them to that goal. "He who thinketh he leadeth and hath no one following him is only out for a walk." John Maxwell has made that concept famous. It is a very humorous way to articulate a difficult and sometimes painful truth. If you're a genuine leader, you will quite naturally attract followers. The problem is that too many of us want a title, but we don't want what comes with leadership. Things like responsibility, conflict and accountability to name a few. Being in the lead puts you on the front line of the battle; it means you are the #1 target; it makes you, by definition, responsible! If it was in my power to do so, I would make each of you the leader of something big for at least two months of your life. It's not all fun and games like most have come to believe and it certainly is not about telling others what to do, and them doing it.

Please notice what Paul had to say about authority (leadership) in the Kingdom of God in II Cor. 10:8: "For though I should boast somewhat more of the authority, which the Lord hath given us for edification, and not for your destruction, I should not be ashamed:" Do you see the difference in this description and what most leadership looks like today? God gives you the authority you have, and it's not from any man. This simple truth has wide ranging ramifications that we may look at later. He also stated that this authority that God has given us is for the edifying of others, and is NOT for their destruction, but is for building them up, and not tearing them down!

Leadership is ultimately about serving others by using your God given gifts and talents, to benefit the team. To build a great team there must be a great leader, someone who knows how to get others to join the team and use their gifts and talents to benefit the team. I serve a great leader and he knows how to get the best from his leadership team. He lets us excel in our God-given talents and encourages us to grow; as we grow he is not intimidated by it, but honored. This is very rare in the ministry, where petty jealousies and pride often keep leaders from pushing people to the top.

This is ironic and disappointing because that's exactly what Paul was trying to communicate when he said that the authority which God gave him was for our "edification." The word here literally means to build up higher and higher like an edifice! We understand this concept with amazing clarity in the raising of our children. How do we get a child to walk, or talk, or anything else? Do we spank them or yell at them until they can do these things perfectly? Of course not, or they would never learn to walk, talk or do anything we wish for them to do. We build them up and cheer them on; we in essence, edify them! When they take one small step, everyone cheers and claps and picks them up and showers them with praises. Yeah, "good girl" or "good boy," mommy loves you so much; that's daddy's precious girl. Then they take two steps, then three, all the while we are building them up, encouraging them, and even comforting them through failures, with what? You guessed it, edification! If our child does something better than us, and we're upset about it, we need to repent. Our ultimate goal and a real leader's greatest legacy would be if we could leave this earth with the knowledge that we helped others become the best they could be. That we were a great enough leader that we, on purpose pushed others to the top! I hope it becomes your greatest joy as well!

1st Cor. 11:1 "Be ye followers of me, even as I also am of Christ." This is a key to having great followers; it sounds simple but, you must be a great follower! The Kingdom of God is based on sowing and reaping, and here's another example. Paul says in this verse, if we follow Christ, we can expect and even invite others to follow just as he did. What amazes me is how many leaders openly disobey God and refuse to listen to those over them, but then expect to reap something completely different!

Leadership whether you realize it or not, is about leading others in what you desire them to do. Simply put, you're sowing what you want to reap. This could be great news or terrible news, depending on what you've sown. Leadership is so difficult to simply define, as a matter of fact, just try to find a definition that any two leaders agree upon, and you will find it's easier to find a needle in a haystack. Here are just a few commonly used descriptions: Visionary, Mentor Counselor, Administrator. Team Builder, Equipper, Peace Maker, the Head, Teacher, Commander, Guide, Director, Authority, Influencer, Supporter, Comforter, Servant, Momentum Starter, Initiator, Pathfinder, and Coach.

I have heard leaders give a glib and quaint simplistic definition for leadership, and then spend the rest of an entire book, or message using many of these other leadership definitions to describe their one simplistic definition. A leader is all these things and much more; they are whatever it takes to keep the ministry heading in the right direction. Ministry is unlike any other vocation on the planet; it has natural elements to it, but it is also a supernatural calling with spiritual elements and spiritual enemies, as well. There is no natural talent that can prepare us for the spiritual battle we call ministry! Paul said in II Cor. 10:4 that we had weapons for this battle, but that they were not carnal weapons. So, while many of our natural leaders can show us wonderful truths about leadership, they could never replace the God-given examples we have in scripture and history. I have probably read as many books on leadership as most of you reading this book, and while I have learned a great deal from these books, none compare to the Bible for it's insights into true leadership.

Early in his career General Norman Schwarzkopf found himself in the middle of an enemy minefield with one of his team injured by a detonated mine. It was here that he showed what made him a great leader. What did he do? Believing the man could survive his injury and even keep his leg, only if he stopped flailing around. He walked across that minefield and pinned the wounded man, then calmed him down. While this is real leadership in action, it falls short of hearing God tell you to send the choir into the battle first, like in II Chron. Chapter 20:20-24. There is no natural leader on the planet that would consider that a good battle strategy; yet, if it's the word of the Lord, it's a great battle plan. Read the encounter and you'll see what I mean. All the leadership skills on the planet will never replace obedience to God's Word. The greatest truth you can know as a spiritual leader, in the ministry, is "it's God who builds his church," and the best you can do is stay out of his way by being obedient.

CHAPTER 12
Faithful Rewards
Sowing to your future success

I f you've read this far, you mean business; you have endured some in-your-face truths and been challenged to the point of offense. This is why I believe I can now share this truth with you and you will embrace, receive, and apply it! Read these passages with me, we will break it down later.

"He that is faithful in that which is least is faithful also in much: and he that is unjust in the least is unjust also in much. If therefore ye have not been faithful in the unrighteous mammon, (money) **who will commit to your trust the true riches? And if ye have not been faithful in that which is another man's, who shall give you that which is your own?"** (Luke 16:10-12).

My goodness, what an incredible set of verses! Notice first of all in verse 10, that money and how you handle money is a test. God is watching how you handle money: are you faithful or unfaithful? If you are faithful,

God can then trust you with something worth far more than the money, "True Riches". He's talking about spiritual riches; supernatural wisdom, spiritual insight, discernment, power, authority, and the operation of the gifts in your life, flowing in the things of God. These are things money can never buy! Check out Acts 8:18-20 and you'll see what I mean. If being faithful with money was so easy, how come so many people fail this test? Being faithful to pay your tithes, when the economy is collapsing around you, faithful to give when the tithe check becomes more than your whole check used to be, faithful with the bosse's credit card, or gas card, or even cash money. People fail this test every day, and miss out on the true riches God really had for them. The true riches of God will lead you to all the other riches of life, "Beloved, I wish above all things that thou mayest prosper and be in health, even as thy soul prospereth" 3rd John 1:2. Matt.6:33 tell us, "But seek ye first the kingdom of God, and his righteousness; and all these things shall be added unto you." Notice he didn't say we're not supposed to seek these things, or that it's wrong for us to want these things; He just said seek the kingdom and God's righteousness first. Then he'll add unto us all the things that the others seek (that God knows we have need of) Matt. 6:32.

I don't want us to get bogged down here, so please just let God reveal to you His desire concerning you and prosperity. The main thing I want you to see is that God is good with you having things; just don't let things have you. The best way to do that is to keep seeking first the Kingdom of God and His righteousness; to keep your mind on things that are above and to be spiritually minded. Once you demonstrate faithfulness in the area of finances, God can do what He's wanted to do from the beginning-give you what he considers "true riches". I love the idea that what most of mankind is so interested in and dedicated to getting more of, God considers a test and only a test. It is the pre-cursor to something He considers far more important: spiritual truths and insights, the ability to be lead by his spirit and to hear his voice saying "this is the way, walk ye in it".

Here's the crème-de-la-crème, in these verses. How you handle someone else's stuff will affect the stuff that's yours! Read verse 12 again, "and if ye have not been faithful in that which belongs to another (their ministry, their anointing, their honor, their favor) who will give you that which is your own?" The answer is "no one"! Whether you realize it or not, what you do with, and how you handle someone else's ministry is sowing to your future. What you sow is what you reap, period! How do you want those who will one day follow you, to serve you? Do you want loyalty, faithfulness, and commitment? Would you like warriors in the faith who would break through enemy lines and then back again just to bring you a glass of water? Do you want individuals with genuine servant's heart for you and the people? Then sow to that with the leader you're serving now; be faithful to honor him and do nothing to dishonor him, even if it will, for the moment, make you look good. Refuse to be someone who murmurs, complains and is critical of the decisions being made. Remember, what you sow is what you'll reap, and if you want what belongs to you, the true riches, you must be faithful with what belongs to another.

That's because in truth "everything" belongs to God; even what you might call your ministry and your anointing, in reality, all belongs to God! If you are faithful with what belongs to another (the little) He will make you ruler of much (the true riches).

What if your leader has some, shall we say, "character flaws"? How can God supply your needs with a leader who is unwilling to help you, unwilling to push you to the top? How can God help without you leaving or promoting yourself? I'm glad you asked, because we have a great example of just how God can do that. We read in Num. 20:8-11 about Moses getting angry at the children of God. This time he was angry because the children of Israel were murmuring and complaining about their need for water! God told Moses to "speak" to the rock, but Moses was angry and struck the rock instead. Even though Moses disobeyed God because he was angry, when he struck the rock water came fourth anyway! What a beautiful example of God's goodness and ability to work through the flaws and mistakes of those over us. His plan to get us what we need is not stopped by our leader's personal flaws or mistakes. Always remember promotion in the Kingdom comes from God and not man; it is God who lifts up and puts down (Psalm 75:6, 7). Our trust must be in the providence of God and not in the provision of man. Then and only then can you serve a man or a ministry with a pure heart, and see the true riches that God wants to give you!

Epilogue

Well there it is – "The Gut Wrenching, Blood, Sweat, and Tears Way to Build a Church." It is my sincere desire that the principles and truths in this book help you and your ministry teams excel in whatever God has called you to do. I have chosen to deal with issues that are strangely missing from most leadership materials. This is not necessarily because they do not know about these issues, or because they are so complicated. Very few people will address these issues – not because they are difficult to teach – because they are difficult to live. Oh, there is also the chance that you will not be invited to any popular Christian TV program any time soon.

While these teachings are simple, that in no way means they are easy to walk out. Simple and easy are not necessarily synonymous. Almost all Biblical teachings are simple. Unconditional love, forgiveness, and submission are all simple concepts to teach, but as anyone who has tried to live by them can tell you, they are far from easy to do.

I have endeavored to share what needs to be said instead of what people want to hear. This is not popular and goes against the countless quick and easy, idiot's guide type of books available to us today. Experience has shown me that the only thing quick and easy in the ministry is failing! It's very disappointing and almost insulting to hear people talk about pastors and Christian leaders as if they're all college dropouts who are incapable of doing anything else – when in truth, many of these leaders are some of the sharpest, most intellectual individuals on the planet! That is why you will never see a serious book called the "Idiot's Guide" to ministry. That is also why I chose to title the book what I did. It is quite honestly "The Gut Wrenching, Blood, Sweat and Tears Way to Build a Church."

Thank you for reading this book, and I pray that it is a blessing to you and your team.

In Christ/Pastor Lee

Index

LS-05 Team Ministry- Building a Dream Team
LS-06 Pride- The Enemy Of Promotion
LS-07 Authority
LS-08 Principle of A Successful Ministry
LS-09 Servant-Style Leadership
LS-10 How to Achieve Excellence 1 & 2
LS-11 Men of Valour & War 1 & 2
LS-12 Spiritual & Church Growth
LS-13 Laws Of Progression
LS-14 Blessed Are The Pure In Heart
LS-15 Successful Christian Leadership
LS-16 The Road To Promotion
LS-17 Enlarging Your Heart & Territory
LS-18 Get Wisdom- & Get Understanding
LS-19 Financial Success
LS-20 Building Significant Churches, "Being A Wise Master Builder"
LS-21 10 Basic Principles of Leadership
LS-22 Enduring Hardship in Ministry
(Ask for a catalog of all the teachings)

About the Author

The author has over 35 years in various leadership positions. The last 25 years have been directly involved with teaching and training servant style leadership. The author now oversees pastors and leaders in multiple locations. He is also involved in ministering to and helping countless other churches through leadership meetings and teaching C/D's.